EMMANUEL JOSEPH

Worldview Marketing, Unlocking the Secrets to Universal Brand Appeal

Copyright © 2025 by Emmanuel Joseph

All rights reserved. No part of this publication may be reproduced, stored or transmitted in any form or by any means, electronic, mechanical, photocopying, recording, scanning, or otherwise without written permission from the publisher. It is illegal to copy this book, post it to a website, or distribute it by any other means without permission.

First edition

This book was professionally typeset on Reedsy.
Find out more at reedsy.com

Contents

1	Chapter 1: The Evolution of Worldview Marketing	1
2	Chapter 2: The Power of Cultural Intelligence	3
3	Chapter 3: Crafting Authentic Brand Narratives	5
4	Chapter 4: Emotional Resonance in Marketing	7
5	Chapter 5: The Role of Social Responsibility	9
6	Chapter 6: Leveraging Digital Engagement	11
7	Chapter 7: The Importance of Brand Consistency	13
8	Chapter 8: Understanding Consumer Psychology	15
9	Chapter 9: Building Trust and Credibility	17
10	Chapter 10: The Art of Cross-Cultural Communication	19
11	Chapter 11: Harnessing the Power of Innovation	21
12	Chapter 12: Measuring Success in Worldview Marketing	23
13	Chapter 13: Navigating Ethical Dilemmas	25
14	Chapter 14: The Future of Worldview Marketing	27
15	Chapter 15: Embracing a Holistic Approach	29

1

Chapter 1: The Evolution of Worldview Marketing

Marketing has been a cornerstone of commerce since the first goods were traded. In the modern era, however, the landscape of marketing has transformed dramatically. The rise of globalization has blurred the lines between markets, making it essential for brands to resonate with diverse audiences. This evolution has given birth to the concept of worldview marketing—a strategic approach that goes beyond traditional marketing tactics to engage audiences on a deeper, more universal level. The key to successful worldview marketing lies in understanding the cultural, social, and emotional contexts that shape consumer behavior across different regions.

To unlock the secrets of universal brand appeal, it's crucial to first grasp the fundamental shifts in consumer mindset. Today's consumers are more connected and informed than ever before. The internet and social media have created a global village where ideas, trends, and values spread rapidly across borders. This interconnectedness means that brands can no longer rely on a one-size-fits-all approach. Instead, they must craft messages that resonate with the unique worldviews of diverse consumer groups while maintaining a consistent brand identity.

Moreover, the concept of authenticity has become a critical component of worldview marketing. Consumers are increasingly skeptical of traditional advertising and are drawn to brands that demonstrate genuine values and social responsibility. Brands that can authentically convey their mission and values while respecting the cultural nuances of their target markets are more likely to build lasting relationships with consumers. This requires a deep understanding of the cultural landscapes in which a brand operates and the ability to tailor messages that resonate on an emotional level.

Finally, effective worldview marketing involves leveraging the power of storytelling. Stories have a unique ability to transcend cultural barriers and connect with people on a personal level. By weaving compelling narratives that reflect the values, aspirations, and experiences of diverse audiences, brands can create a sense of belonging and loyalty among consumers. In the chapters that follow, we will explore the various strategies and techniques that brands can use to unlock the secrets of universal brand appeal, from cultural intelligence and emotional resonance to digital engagement and social impact.

2

Chapter 2: The Power of Cultural Intelligence

In a world where cultural diversity is both celebrated and complex, cultural intelligence has become an invaluable asset for marketers. Cultural intelligence, or CQ, refers to the ability to understand, respect, and effectively navigate different cultural contexts. It's not just about knowing cultural norms and customs, but also about recognizing the deeper values and beliefs that drive consumer behavior. For brands aiming to achieve universal appeal, developing a high CQ is essential.

At the heart of cultural intelligence is empathy—the ability to see the world through the eyes of others. This means going beyond surface-level observations and striving to understand the underlying motivations and emotions of different cultural groups. By fostering empathy, marketers can create campaigns that resonate on a personal level and build genuine connections with diverse audiences. Empathy also enables brands to avoid cultural missteps and navigate sensitive issues with grace and respect.

Another critical aspect of cultural intelligence is adaptability. In a globalized marketplace, brands must be agile and responsive to the ever-changing cultural landscape. This involves staying attuned to emerging trends, shifts in consumer sentiment, and the impact of social and political events on different cultural groups. By staying adaptable, brands can ensure their messages remain relevant and impactful across diverse markets. This flexibility allows brands to pivot their strategies when necessary and embrace new opportunities for growth.

Finally, cultural intelligence requires a commitment to continuous learning. The world is constantly evolving, and so too are the cultural contexts in which brands operate. Marketers must be proactive in expanding their cultural knowledge and staying informed about the latest developments in their target markets. This can be achieved through ongoing education, immersive experiences, and collaboration with local experts and influencers. By embracing a mindset of lifelong learning, brands can maintain their cultural relevance and build enduring relationships with consumers around the world.

3

Chapter 3: Crafting Authentic Brand Narratives

In an era where consumers are bombarded with an overwhelming amount of information and advertisements, authenticity has emerged as a key differentiator for brands. Authentic brand narratives go beyond promotional messages and instead focus on telling genuine stories that reflect a brand's core values, mission, and identity. These narratives resonate with consumers on an emotional level and foster trust and loyalty. To craft authentic brand narratives, marketers must first understand the essence of their brand and the unique value it brings to the world.

The foundation of an authentic brand narrative is a clear and compelling brand story. This story should articulate the brand's origin, purpose, and vision in a way that is relatable and inspiring. It's not just about highlighting the products or services a brand offers, but also about conveying the passion, dedication, and values that drive the brand. By sharing the journey behind the brand, marketers can create a sense of connection and empathy with consumers, making them feel like they are part of the brand's story.

Another important element of an authentic brand narrative is transparency. In today's digital age, consumers have access to a wealth of information and are quick to call out brands that are perceived as dishonest or insincere. To build credibility, brands must be transparent about their practices, values, and impact. This includes being open about the challenges they face and the steps they are taking to address them. By demonstrating honesty and integrity, brands can earn the trust and respect of their audience.

Moreover, authentic brand narratives should be inclusive and reflect the diverse experiences and perspectives of their audience. This means acknowledging and celebrating the unique cultural, social, and personal backgrounds of consumers. By embracing diversity and inclusion, brands can create narratives that resonate with a wide range of audiences and foster a sense of belonging. Inclusive narratives also help to break down stereotypes and promote positive social change.

4

Chapter 4: Emotional Resonance in Marketing

Emotions are at the core of human experience and play a significant role in consumer decision-making. Emotional resonance in marketing involves creating messages that evoke strong emotions and connect with consumers on a personal level. This approach goes beyond rational appeals and taps into the feelings and desires that drive behavior. To achieve emotional resonance, brands must understand the emotional landscape of their target audience and craft messages that speak to their hopes, fears, and aspirations.

One of the most effective ways to create emotional resonance is through storytelling. Stories have the power to evoke emotions, create empathy, and leave a lasting impression. By sharing relatable and compelling narratives, brands can connect with consumers on a deeper level and inspire loyalty. Whether it's a heartwarming tale of a customer overcoming challenges or an inspiring story of the brand's journey, storytelling can make marketing messages more engaging and memorable.

Another key aspect of emotional resonance is personalization. In a world where consumers are inundated with generic advertisements, personalized messages stand out and make a meaningful impact. By leveraging data and insights, brands can tailor their messages to the unique preferences and needs of individual consumers. Personalization goes beyond addressing consumers by their names; it involves understanding their interests, behaviors, and emotions. When consumers feel that a brand understands and cares about them, they are more likely to develop a strong emotional connection.

Visual and sensory elements also play a crucial role in creating emotional resonance. The use of colors, imagery, music, and even scents can evoke specific emotions and enhance the overall impact of a marketing campaign. For example, warm colors like red and orange can create a sense of excitement and urgency, while cool colors like blue and green can evoke feelings of calm and trust. By carefully selecting visual and sensory elements that align with the desired emotional response, brands can create a more immersive and impactful experience for consumers.

5

Chapter 5: The Role of Social Responsibility

In today's socially conscious world, consumers expect brands to do more than just sell products; they want brands to make a positive impact on society. Social responsibility has become a critical component of modern marketing, as consumers increasingly seek out brands that align with their values and contribute to the greater good. To build universal brand appeal, marketers must integrate social responsibility into their strategies and demonstrate a genuine commitment to making a difference.

One way to showcase social responsibility is through cause marketing. This involves partnering with charitable organizations, supporting social causes, or launching initiatives that address pressing issues such as climate change, poverty, or inequality. By aligning with causes that resonate with their target audience, brands can build a sense of purpose and foster loyalty among consumers who share similar values. It's essential for brands to be authentic in their efforts and avoid superficial gestures, as consumers are quick to recognize and call out insincerity.

Another important aspect of social responsibility is sustainability. Consumers are increasingly concerned about the environmental impact of their purchases and are drawn to brands that prioritize sustainability. This includes adopting eco-friendly practices, reducing waste, and using ethically sourced materials. By transparently communicating their sustainability efforts and progress, brands can build trust and credibility with environmentally conscious consumers.

Employee welfare and ethical business practices are also key components of social responsibility. Brands that treat their employees fairly, promote diversity and inclusion, and operate with integrity are more likely to earn the respect and loyalty of their audience. By prioritizing the well-being of their workforce and conducting business ethically, brands can create a positive reputation and build long-lasting relationships with consumers.

6

Chapter 6: Leveraging Digital Engagement

In the digital age, the ways consumers interact with brands have transformed significantly. Digital engagement involves creating meaningful and interactive experiences across various digital platforms. This can include social media, websites, mobile apps, and more. To unlock universal brand appeal, marketers must leverage digital engagement to build connections, foster loyalty, and create value for consumers.

Social media has become a powerful tool for digital engagement. Platforms like Facebook, Instagram, Twitter, and TikTok offer unique opportunities for brands to reach and engage with their audience. By creating compelling content, engaging with followers, and participating in conversations, brands can build a vibrant online community. Social media also allows for real-time interactions, enabling brands to respond to customer inquiries, gather feedback, and show appreciation for their audience.

Another key aspect of digital engagement is creating a seamless and user-friendly online experience. This involves optimizing websites and mobile apps to ensure they are easy to navigate, visually appealing, and provide valuable content. A positive online experience can enhance brand perception and encourage repeat visits. Additionally, incorporating interactive elements such as quizzes, surveys, and gamification can make the digital experience more engaging and enjoyable for consumers.

Personalization is also crucial for effective digital engagement. By leveraging data and analytics, brands can deliver personalized content and recommendations that cater to the individual preferences and needs of their audience. This can include personalized emails, targeted advertisements, and customized website experiences. When consumers feel that a brand understands and caters to their unique needs, they are more likely to develop a strong emotional connection and loyalty.

7

Chapter 7: The Importance of Brand Consistency

Consistency is a key factor in building a strong and recognizable brand. Brand consistency involves maintaining a cohesive and uniform message, tone, and visual identity across all marketing channels and touchpoints. This consistency helps to reinforce brand identity, build trust, and create a memorable brand experience for consumers. To achieve universal brand appeal, marketers must prioritize brand consistency in their strategies.

A consistent brand message ensures that consumers receive the same core values and promises regardless of where or how they interact with the brand. This can be achieved by developing clear brand guidelines that outline the brand's mission, values, tone of voice, and visual elements. By adhering to these guidelines, marketers can ensure that all marketing materials, from advertisements to social media posts, align with the brand's identity.

Visual consistency is also essential for reinforcing brand recognition. This includes using the same colors, fonts, logos, and design elements across all marketing materials. A consistent visual identity helps consumers easily identify the brand and associate it with positive experiences. Additionally, maintaining visual consistency across different cultural contexts requires careful consideration of cultural nuances and preferences.

Tone of voice consistency is another important aspect of brand consistency. The way a brand communicates with its audience should reflect its personality and values. Whether the tone is friendly, professional, humorous, or inspirational, it should remain consistent across all communications. This helps to create a cohesive brand experience and build trust with consumers.

8

Chapter 8: Understanding Consumer Psychology

To unlock the secrets of universal brand appeal, marketers must understand the psychological factors that influence consumer behavior. Consumer psychology involves studying how thoughts, feelings, and perceptions impact purchasing decisions. By gaining insights into consumer psychology, brands can develop strategies that effectively resonate with their audience and drive engagement.

One of the key principles of consumer psychology is the concept of motivation. Consumers are driven by various motivations, such as the desire for status, the need for convenience, or the pursuit of happiness. By understanding the underlying motivations of their target audience, brands can craft messages that appeal to these desires and create a sense of urgency.

Another important aspect of consumer psychology is perception. Perception refers to how consumers interpret and make sense of information. This can be influenced by factors such as past experiences, cultural background, and social influences. Brands can shape consumer perceptions by carefully designing their messaging, packaging, and overall brand experience. Creating positive associations and managing consumer expectations can enhance brand perception and drive loyalty.

Emotion also plays a significant role in consumer decision-making. Emotions can influence how consumers perceive a brand, recall information, and make purchasing decisions. By creating emotionally charged marketing campaigns, brands can evoke feelings of joy, excitement, nostalgia, or empathy. Emotional appeals can create a strong connection with consumers and increase the likelihood of brand loyalty.

9

Chapter 9: Building Trust and Credibility

Trust and credibility are the cornerstones of a successful brand. In an age where consumers are more discerning and skeptical than ever, building and maintaining trust is crucial for achieving universal brand appeal. Trust is earned over time through consistent actions, transparency, and delivering on promises. Credibility, on the other hand, is established by demonstrating expertise, reliability, and authenticity.

One of the most effective ways to build trust is through transparent communication. Brands that are open and honest about their practices, values, and intentions are more likely to earn the trust of their audience. This includes being upfront about product ingredients, sourcing methods, and any potential risks or limitations. Transparency also involves acknowledging and addressing mistakes or challenges. By taking responsibility and communicating openly, brands can demonstrate integrity and build credibility.

Another important aspect of building trust is consistency. Consistent actions and messaging reinforce the brand's identity and reliability. When consumers experience consistency across all touchpoints—whether it's in marketing materials, customer service interactions, or product quality—they are more likely to develop trust in the brand. Consistency also helps to establish a strong brand identity and create a sense of familiarity and reliability.

Third-party endorsements and social proof can also enhance credibility.

Positive reviews, testimonials, and endorsements from industry experts or influencers can validate the brand's claims and build trust among consumers. Additionally, partnerships with reputable organizations and participation in industry certifications can further establish the brand's credibility. By leveraging social proof and third-party endorsements, brands can enhance their reputation and gain the trust of their audience.

10

Chapter 10: The Art of Cross-Cultural Communication

Cross-cultural communication is a critical skill for marketers aiming to achieve universal brand appeal. It involves understanding and effectively navigating the cultural differences that exist between various consumer groups. Effective cross-cultural communication requires cultural sensitivity, adaptability, and a deep understanding of the cultural contexts in which the brand operates.

Cultural sensitivity is the foundation of cross-cultural communication. It involves recognizing and respecting the cultural norms, values, and beliefs of different consumer groups. This means being aware of potential cultural taboos, avoiding stereotypes, and showing genuine respect for cultural diversity. By demonstrating cultural sensitivity, brands can create messages that resonate with diverse audiences and avoid unintentional offense.

Adaptability is another key component of cross-cultural communication. Brands must be flexible and willing to adjust their messaging and strategies to fit the cultural nuances of different markets. This may involve tailoring language, imagery, and tone to align with cultural preferences and expectations. Adaptability also means staying attuned to changes in the cultural landscape and being responsive to emerging trends and shifts in consumer sentiment.

Building cultural competence through continuous learning is essential for effective cross-cultural communication. Marketers must invest time and effort in understanding the cultural contexts of their target markets. This can be achieved through research, immersion, and collaboration with local experts and influencers. By continuously expanding their cultural knowledge, brands can create more relevant and impactful messages that resonate with diverse audiences.

11

Chapter 11: Harnessing the Power of Innovation

Innovation is a driving force behind successful marketing strategies. In a rapidly changing world, brands must continuously innovate to stay ahead of the competition and meet the evolving needs of consumers. Innovation involves thinking creatively, embracing new technologies, and finding unique ways to engage and delight consumers.

One way to harness the power of innovation is by leveraging technology. Advances in digital technology, artificial intelligence, and data analytics have opened up new opportunities for brands to connect with consumers. From personalized marketing campaigns to immersive virtual experiences, technology can enhance the overall brand experience and create memorable interactions. Brands that embrace technology and stay ahead of digital trends can gain a competitive edge and captivate their audience.

Creative thinking and experimentation are also essential for innovation. Brands must be willing to take risks, explore new ideas, and push the boundaries of traditional marketing. This involves fostering a culture of creativity within the organization and encouraging employees to think outside the box. By experimenting with new concepts and approaches, brands can discover innovative solutions that resonate with consumers and drive engagement.

Collaboration and partnerships can further fuel innovation. By working with other organizations, startups, or industry experts, brands can gain fresh perspectives and access new resources. Collaborative innovation can lead to the development of groundbreaking products, services, and marketing campaigns. Brands that actively seek out and embrace collaboration are more likely to stay at the forefront of innovation and create a lasting impact.

12

Chapter 12: Measuring Success in Worldview Marketing

Measuring the success of worldview marketing efforts is crucial to understanding their impact and refining strategies for continuous improvement. Traditional metrics such as sales figures and market share remain important, but they must be complemented by more nuanced indicators that capture the effectiveness of cross-cultural and emotionally resonant campaigns. In this chapter, we'll explore various methods and tools for evaluating the success of worldview marketing initiatives.

One of the key metrics to consider is brand perception. Brand perception surveys and social listening tools can provide valuable insights into how consumers view a brand across different cultural contexts. By monitoring online conversations, reviews, and social media mentions, marketers can gauge sentiment and identify areas for improvement. Positive changes in brand perception can indicate that a brand's messaging is resonating with its target audience.

Another important metric is engagement. Engagement metrics, such as likes, shares, comments, and click-through rates, can help assess the effectiveness of digital marketing campaigns. High levels of engagement suggest that consumers find the content relevant and compelling. Additionally, tracking customer interactions across various touchpoints can provide a comprehensive view of how consumers are engaging with the brand. This can include website visits, app usage, and participation in loyalty programs.

Customer loyalty and retention are also critical indicators of success. Loyal customers are more likely to make repeat purchases, recommend the brand to others, and provide valuable feedback. Metrics such as customer lifetime value, repeat purchase rate, and net promoter score can help assess the strength of customer loyalty. By fostering strong relationships with consumers and delivering consistent value, brands can build a loyal customer base that drives long-term success.

13

Chapter 13: Navigating Ethical Dilemmas

In the pursuit of universal brand appeal, marketers may encounter ethical dilemmas that require careful consideration and decision-making. Navigating these dilemmas with integrity and transparency is essential for maintaining consumer trust and upholding the brand's values. This chapter will explore common ethical challenges in marketing and provide guidance on how to address them.

One of the most pressing ethical issues in marketing is data privacy. With the increasing use of data to personalize marketing efforts, brands must ensure they are collecting, storing, and using consumer data responsibly. This includes obtaining informed consent, being transparent about data usage, and implementing robust security measures to protect consumer information. Brands that prioritize data privacy and respect consumer rights are more likely to build trust and credibility.

Another ethical challenge is the potential for cultural appropriation. Cultural appropriation occurs when elements of one culture are used by another culture, often without permission or proper understanding. This can lead to misrepresentation and offense. To navigate this challenge, brands must approach cultural themes with sensitivity and respect. This involves collaborating with cultural experts, seeking input from diverse voices, and ensuring that cultural elements are used in an authentic and meaningful way.

Greenwashing, or the practice of making misleading claims about a brand's environmental efforts, is another ethical concern. Consumers are increasingly demanding transparency and authenticity in sustainability claims. Brands must ensure that their environmental initiatives are genuine and backed by evidence. By providing clear and accurate information about their sustainability efforts, brands can build trust and avoid accusations of greenwashing.

14

Chapter 14: The Future of Worldview Marketing

As the world continues to evolve, so too will the landscape of marketing. The future of worldview marketing will be shaped by emerging trends, technological advancements, and shifting consumer expectations. In this chapter, we'll explore some of the key trends and developments that are likely to influence the future of worldview marketing.

One of the most significant trends is the rise of artificial intelligence (AI) and machine learning. These technologies are transforming the way brands analyze data, personalize experiences, and engage with consumers. AI-powered tools can help marketers gain deeper insights into consumer behavior, optimize marketing strategies, and deliver highly targeted content. As AI continues to advance, it will play an increasingly important role in shaping the future of marketing.

Another key trend is the growing importance of social impact and purpose-driven marketing. Consumers are increasingly looking for brands that align with their values and contribute to positive social change. Brands that embrace social impact initiatives and demonstrate a genuine commitment to making a difference will be well-positioned to attract and retain loyal customers. This trend is likely to continue as consumers become more socially conscious and demand greater accountability from brands.

The future of worldview marketing will also be influenced by advancements in digital and immersive technologies. Virtual reality (VR), augmented reality (AR), and other immersive experiences offer new opportunities for brands to engage with consumers in innovative ways. These technologies can create memorable and interactive experiences that resonate with diverse audiences and enhance brand perception.

15

Chapter 15: Embracing a Holistic Approach

To unlock the secrets to universal brand appeal, marketers must embrace a holistic approach that integrates cultural intelligence, emotional resonance, social responsibility, digital engagement, and innovation. This final chapter will recap the key principles and strategies discussed throughout the book and provide actionable insights for implementing a successful worldview marketing strategy.

At the core of a holistic approach is a deep understanding of the diverse cultural contexts in which a brand operates. By developing cultural intelligence and fostering empathy, brands can create messages that resonate with diverse audiences and build genuine connections. This requires ongoing learning, adaptability, and collaboration with cultural experts.

Emotional resonance is also essential for creating meaningful and lasting relationships with consumers. By crafting authentic brand narratives, leveraging storytelling, and personalizing experiences, brands can connect with consumers on an emotional level. This emotional connection drives loyalty and advocacy.

Social responsibility must be integrated into every aspect of a brand's strategy. By prioritizing sustainability, ethical practices, and social impact, brands can build trust and credibility with socially conscious consumers.

This commitment to social responsibility enhances brand reputation and contributes to positive social change.

Digital engagement and innovation are key drivers of success in the modern marketing landscape. By embracing new technologies, creating seamless online experiences, and experimenting with creative ideas, brands can stay ahead of the competition and captivate their audience.

Ultimately, a holistic approach to worldview marketing requires a commitment to continuous improvement and a willingness to evolve with the changing world. By staying attuned to consumer needs, cultural shifts, and emerging trends, brands can unlock the secrets to universal brand appeal and achieve long-term success.

Book Description

In today's interconnected world, the quest for universal brand appeal is more important—and challenging—than ever. "Worldview Marketing: Unlocking the Secrets to Universal Brand Appeal" takes readers on a journey through the evolving landscape of global marketing. This insightful book delves into the principles of cultural intelligence, emotional resonance, and social responsibility, providing a comprehensive guide for brands aiming to connect with diverse audiences.

The book explores the power of authentic storytelling and the importance of building trust and credibility in a skeptical world. It offers practical strategies for digital engagement and innovation, while emphasizing the need for a holistic approach that integrates empathy, adaptability, and continuous learning. From navigating ethical dilemmas to measuring success, "Worldview Marketing" equips marketers with the tools and knowledge to thrive in a global marketplace.

Whether you're a seasoned marketer or a newcomer to the field, this book provides valuable insights and actionable advice to help you craft messages that resonate across cultural boundaries and create meaningful connections with consumers. Discover the secrets to unlocking universal brand appeal and transforming your marketing efforts with "Worldview Marketing."

www.ingramcontent.com/pod-product-compliance
Lightning Source LLC
Chambersburg PA
CBHW050156130526
44590CB00044B/3368